MONDAY

MORNING

COMMUNICATIONS

Eight Lessons ... Great Results

David Cottrell, Tony Jeary & George Lowe

CornerStone
Leadership Institute

www.**cornerstoneleadership**.com

MONDAY
MORNING
COMMUNICATIONS

Eight Lessons ... Great Results

Inquiries regarding permission for use of the material contained in this book should be addressed to:
CornerStone Leadership Institute
P.O. Box 764087
Dallas, TX 75376
888.789.LEAD

Printed in the United States of America
ISBN: 0-9762528-3-X

Credits
Design, art direction, and production   Back Porch Creative, Plano, TX

Table of Contents

Prologue

*J*eni Johnson, eighteen months ago...

I could not believe what I was reading as I looked over the employee survey!

- ♦ "I never know what's going on around here."
- ♦ "I'm buried in unimportant e-mail, yet not copied on critical items when I need to be in the loop."
- ♦ "I get too many phone calls because our intranet site is not working, bulletins are not clear and e-mails are often confusing or untimely."
- ♦ "People are not clear about what they want."
- ♦ "Presentations are often poorly organized and meetings are frequently a waste of time."
- ♦ "I get too many confusing or conflicting communications and can rarely figure out exactly what I'm supposed to do."

Overall, the survey results were excellent but my team's comments about communications made it obvious I was not doing a great job. I was stunned by what I read as I sat in the coffee lounge that day.

How had communications become such a problem? I consider myself an excellent communicator and spend considerable time on my messages in an effort to be as clear as possible. Obviously, something was missing.

As I began to deal with my bruised ego, Michael, one of my peers and a good friend, walked in with a cup of coffee and a long face.

Before I could say a word, he whispered, "You will not believe what my team said on my survey. Overall, my numbers were good, but in one area …."

I interrupted his sentence, "Let me guess – communications?"

"Right … can you believe that? As much time and energy as we spend trying to get the word out … developing resources, leaving voice mails, sending e-mails and conducting meetings and conference calls … how could communications be an issue? How can I possibly do more? I wear myself out communicating as it is."

Just then, Jeff Walters, our former boss walked in. Jeff had been promoted to head up a new division. Earlier, he had worked with Michael and me, helping get us promotions to our first management positions. We asked him to join us.

Jeff immediately sensed something was wrong and in his normal, no-nonsense style, cut to the chase. "You both look like you've just lost your best friend."

We showed him the employee survey results we had just received.

"I can't imagine it is about leadership issues," Jeff began.

"No," we said in unison, careful to keep our voices low. "It's something pretty basic: communications!"

It wasn't that we had flunked, mind you, but we did receive grades lower than we expected. On both of our survey reports, communications was the number one area our employees felt needed improvement.

Eager to wipe this blemish from our records, Michael and I both wanted to take immediate action to correct the problems our employees had pointed out.

"I guess I really shouldn't be surprised," I admitted. "I have many of the same concerns myself – and included them on the survey I filled out. But instead of looking in the mirror, I guess I felt I had been taking care of business when it comes to communications."

"You're right," Michael chimed in. "I'm continually frustrated by people who waste my time. I receive too many fuzzy communications, poorly written reports and e-mails that show little understanding of the topic at hand. But when it comes to my communications, I really thought I was connecting better."

"I had some of those same issues, but what I really worried about was the toll these communications problems was taking on my team – and me – in terms of time and effectiveness … not to mention the stress," he said.

"This survey also makes me wonder if poor communications is the reason we're not progressing faster toward our goals," I added.

Michael also thought there may be a connection between poor communications and our often unmanageable workload. "Here's an example," he said. "I continue to prioritize but wind up working late almost every night and spending time every weekend reading e-mails."

"Whoa!" Jeff said, before I could launch into another issue. "I've been down this path before and know pretty much what you're up against. We faced many of the same issues when the employee surveys first came out.

"Based on my experience, the good news is that something can be done and there is something you can do," Jeff continued, "but you have to step up and own the issue!

"A lot of the answers to your team's concerns are common sense. The problem is there are *numerous* common sense items that have to be addressed *at the same time.* You need solutions that will 'stick' and then continue to work."

"Man, that sure loads my plate with things to think about," I said, mulling over his last statement.

"There's one thing I can tell you for sure," Jeff promised. "People really appreciate clear communications. You'll also earn major points from your team for removing some of the roadblocks they have to live with. In other words, guys, while communications problem are serious and complicated, they are problems you **can fix** – and it's worth doing.

"In terms of the specific things you need to do, I have a friend who I believe would be delighted – no, **honored** – to give you some guidance on how to solve these problems."

Michael and I looked at each other and then nodded our interest as Jeff told his story.

"Some years back, I reconnected with Tony Pearce, one of my father's friends and a guy I hadn't seen since I graduated from college.

"Tony is a successful, semi-retired business leader who now spends his time writing books and coaching top executives. I'm not sure of his exact age, but what's important is he has the wisdom and business acumen equivalent to a team of senior advisors.

"I contacted him because I was having some serious doubts about my leadership skills. In a period of eight weeks of Monday Morning meetings, he walked me through a program that was probably the equivalent of a master's degree in leadership. It also was a turning point in my career," Jeff admitted. "It even led me to write a book about it – *Monday Morning Leadership*.

"Tony's not one of those egotistical, self-made millionaires with a 'know it all' attitude. He's a warm, regular guy who's widely respected ... and he gives back to the community – with his time and money – simply because he wants to help others.

"I have used Tony's wisdom as a guide during the past few years and I'm sure if I call him...."

"Please call him!" we interrupted.

Jeff waved as he left the coffee room, promising to call Tony after lunch.

*   *   *

In his conversation with his mentor, Jeff learned that Tony had been out of the country on a book tour, promoting the international release of his latest leadership book.

After setting a date to have breakfast, Jeff filled Tony in on the employee survey and the challenges it had created for Michael and me, suggesting this might be a project he would like to take on … if he had the time.

Tony was willing to help, but he also had questions with regard to our willingness to pass along what we learned from him. As he consented to meet with us, he asked Jeff to gain our commitment to some active teaching, or perhaps as Jeff had done, to write a book on the subject after our Monday morning sessions were completed.

Jeff was confident we would agree to Tony's requirements and made an appointment for us to begin on Monday the 21st at 8:30.

Later, Jeff met briefly with us to let us know the deal was set – as long as we bought into Tony's requirement to "pass it on."

"No problem," said Michael. "I would love to teach others how to address the same issues we're working on. Count me in."

After a journalism class in college, I had always wanted to write a book, and couldn't help but think our sessions with Tony might just be the book within me that was waiting to be written.

"Okay, then." Jeff seemed pleased he could help us spend some time with Tony. "Be there Monday the 21st, at 8:30. Here are the directions … and to keep me out of trouble, be on time!"

Jeff then gave us copies of his book, *Monday Morning Leadership.* "If you can read this before your first meeting with Tony, it will give you a lead on his background and how he works.

"If you listen to him and act on his advice, it will make a big difference in your career. Enjoy your time with Tony!"

*   *   *

All of us contributing to *Monday Morning Communications* are honored you are investing your time in reading it.

We hope you enjoy the book and simply ask you, in turn, to help others discover the wisdom Tony provides in the following story.

The First Monday

You Touch It,
You Own It

*M*ichael and I had agreed to meet before the first Monday morning session to put together a list of the issues we wanted to address before driving over to Tony's place.

"So Michael, I guess it's natural to be petrified about exposing all of our faults to a person of Tony's stature," I said, as my stomach alternately knotted and unknotted.

"At least what we're going to learn about gives us a little license to be nervous. Even great communicators probably feel anxious before meeting new audiences," Michael said.

Heeding Jeff's warning about being on time for our meetings with Tony, we didn't get to complete our agenda but got most of the important problems written down.

Our list looked like this:

Employee Survey Communications Issues

- Despite our best efforts and intentions, a lot of people still say "I never know what's going on around here."

- Volume of "communications" is too high; clarity and effectiveness, unacceptably low.

- One poor communication can create many other ineffective communications these, in turn, compound problems.

- There may be some culture issues perhaps trust that are in the way of good communications.

- Sometimes we simply don't take enough time to write or speak carefully and clearly.

- Our communications, taken together, often deliver confusing and mixed messages. This results in people doing the wrong thing or wasting time figuring out the right thing to do.

- The impact on us as managers could be severe. As otherwise pretty good leaders, we know this is a problem we must address promptly and effectively.

- On the positive side, if we could improve communications, we might reduce our stress and improve our results.

 We pulled into Tony's driveway at 8:28 that first Monday morning and as we walked toward the door, Michael said he was already getting a positive feeling.

Tony's house was in keeping with his upscale neighborhood, but not pretentious. The winding path to the front door was inviting.

We rang the bell and were greeted with a very warm and enthusiastic, "Good morning and welcome to my home!" from a man wearing an argyle sweater and a grandfatherly reassurance. "You must be the Michael and Jeni I've been anxious to meet!"

"Absolutely," I said, "but I'll bet we're more anxious than you are because of this little, uh, communications pickle we're in."

"Well," said Tony, "we'll dive right into that little pickle shortly, but first I need to give you a quick walk-around and show you where to find the coffee."

Tony's house was impressive, but very warm and welcoming. "This is where we'll be meeting for the next eight weeks," he pointed out as we entered the large study. It looked like a professionally maintained library with its walls lined with thousands of books. The electronics wall had the latest in equipment, hundreds of CDs and DVDs, as well as a corner set up for video conferencing.

Between the shelves, family photos and pictures of Tony with well-known business and political leaders covered most of the remaining open spaces.

We sat down in comfortable leather chairs around a small table at one end of the study and Tony kicked things off by asking us to brief him on our backgrounds.

Next, he recapped his own professional history before opening the work session by saying, "So what brings you here? What specifically are you up against?"

"Frankly Tony," I said, "We were shocked by our team's comments on a recent survey. To our surprise, our team thinks our communications are not connecting with them. So, we are asking for your advice on how to best attack this issue."

"I think you've come to the right place," Tony reassured. "I've had some experiences very similar to what you're working on and I believe I can help.

"One of the keys to dealing positively with your situation is captured in a simple phrase I learned many years ago and that is feedback is the breakfast of champions.

"Let's think about this," Tony continued. "You've received a report card with some disappointing grades, but as long as you do something with the information you have received, you don't need to worry about the low marks. If you harness your fear and anxiety in a positive way, it can be a powerful force, moving you toward solutions.

"However, before we get too far into solutions, I need to go over a few housekeeping items. I've put together a few guidelines for our time together," Tony said.

His handwritten list looked like this:

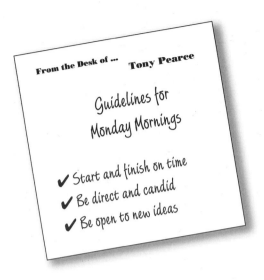

"These look good to me," Michael said, and I nodded in agreement.

"Okay then," Tony said. "Let's start with a basic idea. One of the most dangerous communications shortcuts we take is assuming we're all on the same page when it comes to the meaning of words.

"As an example, you need to make sure you understand the meaning behind the words your employees have used on the survey. Interpreting these words correctly will help you define the problems you need to resolve, and avoid wasting time on blind alleys.

"Let me illustrate my point with a brief story," said Tony. "A client in the automotive industry once told me about a customer who was being asked her opinion of a new vehicle in a market research clinic.

"The woman had looked over the prototype car very carefully and had gotten in and out several times. 'I'm just not sure I would be comfortable in it,' she said. So, the researchers summoned the seating engineers over to hear the rest of her comments.

'Oh no,' she said. 'The seats are just fine. I'm worried about how its bold new styling will fit in with the rest of the cars in my neighborhood, and whether I would be *comfortable* having my conservative friends and neighbors see this car in my driveway.'

"So," Tony smiled, "if you're *comfortable* with this approach, I suggest we begin by agreeing on a meaning for '*communications*.'"

We groaned at the pun, and our humor-driven bonding was underway.

"Communications is such a broad topic, we need to cut it down to a manageable size," Tony began. "I like to think about what you're trying to fix as *Communications That Count* so we can exclude necessary-but-mundane communications like, 'Paper or plastic?' or 'Still raining?'

"To me," he continued, "*Communications That Count* have clear objectives. They are designed to cause action, convey key information and/or change or reinforce others' thinking about important matters.

"Even with this narrow definition, however, we're left with a daunting array of communications each day of every week," he continued. "Add up the phone calls, e-mails, intranet bulletins, meetings, formal presentations and face-to-face contacts you're involved in and you'll be astounded at how many *Communications That Count* you touch.

"There's one more area I want to cover today and it's both complicated and straight forward at the same time. Let me ask you this: who really **owns** a communication within an organization?"

"Well," I ventured, tentatively, "I suppose we all do."

"That's right," Tony replied, "but unless we're talking about a truly global issue, we need to pin it down a bit more ... and please don't take this as personal criticism. I believe there may have been some fundamentals about communicating we didn't pick up on in school, because they typically aren't taught.

"In terms of individual communications, the *sender is primarily responsible* for the success of a communication. If I want you to do something, change your thinking about something or simply want you to come to a meeting tomorrow at 3:00, it's my responsibility to ensure you *receive* my message *in a form* that's readily understood," he explained.

"Call me an old fogey, but if you send me a text message on my cell phone that says something like *Tues 3:00 con call Michael,* I think it's reasonable that I may not know which Tuesday or which Michael (I know 14 of them). For sure, I wouldn't know why I would want to participate in a conference call on an unidentified phone number about a subject that wasn't disclosed!

"At the same time, if someone makes a reasonable attempt to tell me something, I'm not licensed to ignore it because they make a mistake," Tony pointed out. "For example, if I get a note about an event scheduled on Wednesday the 24th, and the 24th falls on a Thursday, it's my responsibility to ask for clarification. Much like the rules of the road, just because you roll through the intersection on a 'pink' light, I don't have the right to smash into you if I can avoid it."

"So," Michael said, "if the senders would take more care and more responsibility, and the receivers would be more curious and forgiving, we could whip most of this problem?"

"That would be a great start," Tony replied, "but as leaders you don't get off the hook that easily. Think of communications in your department where all of the senders and receivers are as pure as the driven snow, yet the combined result is mass confusion."

"The light bulb just came on," Michael announced. "We had one of these just the other day. A situation arose that needed immediate action and two of our unit supervisors got on it right away.

"The problem was that they acted independently. Each one made similar assignments to different people. Needless to say, the people involved in the duplication of effort weren't pleased. The customer wasn't happy, either, because she was getting calls from two people asking the same questions.

"Now that you have provided this perspective, I can think of many other examples," Michael said. It's clear we, as leaders, have important responsibilities for the systems aspects of communications.

"We need to assure there is clarity across the organization and be certain small errors in one area of the system aren't transformed into huge problems, because no one is watching the entire process. Something as simple as getting a date wrong in an initial communication can have an enormous impact if several departments are involved in meeting an important deadline."

"Bingo!" said Tony. "Wrap this all together, and I call it the '*you touch it, you own it*' rule of communications. Simply stated:

Effective Communications Begin with You!

Whether we're senders, receivers or supervisors of a communications process, we *all* have responsibilities to make sure messages are as clear, efficient and effective as they can be.

Tony glanced at his watch. "And, I think I'm going to quit while I'm ahead," he said, "besides, we're about out of time for today. With a chuckle he added, "and I need to let you get back to your real work before you get into **more** trouble. But before you go, I want to give you a 'homework' assignment.

"Between now and next Monday, I'd like for you to study your own *Communications That Count*. Please bring back a report that gives your situation a better focus.

"I'd like a rundown that uses the *Reporter's Questions* – you know, using the 'who, what, where, when, how, how many and why' questions journalists use to get at the core of a story. Over the years, I've found these questions very helpful in looking at all aspects of a matter.

"Especially in the communications area, I find that people often focus too much on the 'what' and 'how' while ignoring the 'who' and 'why' of a situation.

"As part of your report, take a sample of your communications and rate its effectiveness on a scale of 1-10. That will help me get a barometer of how deep your communications ditch might be.

"Also, I'd like to get a feel for the difference in perceptions you have versus what your people perceive – the gap, if you will.

"One more thing – and I promise this is the last one," Tony smiled. "I'd like you to bring an example of what you believe is a really effective communication – and be prepared to explain why it works."

 Tony then handed both of us a spiral notebook with the words "Mondays with Tony" handwritten across the cover. "Take this notebook and begin writing down what we discuss during each of our meetings," he said. "It will be easier for you to keep track of what we have covered."

"So is there anything you will be doing this week to make your situation better?"

"The matter of looking at feedback as the 'breakfast of champions' helps me face this challenge in a whole new light," I said. "I'm also going to stop complaining and turn my energy in a more positive direction, because I'm beginning to recognize *if I touch it, I own it.*"

"I agree with Jeni," Michael said, picking up his own copy of Tony's notebook, "and given the number of *Communications That Count* we are dealing with, I'm going to move this opportunity – fixing our communications problems – way up on my priority list!"

As we said our goodbyes and were walking out the door, Tony turned to us and said, "Thanks again for coming today. I am honored that you've selected me to help guide you on such an important journey."

*   *   *

Later that day, I opened the notebook to record the lessons I had learned. Inside was a note from Tony that confirmed his support and commitment. As I read the note, I felt the genuineness of his words.

As I began to record my thoughts about what I had learned that day, I felt that warm "and away we go" feeling you get when you know you're headed in the right direction ... in good company.

My notes for the day included these:

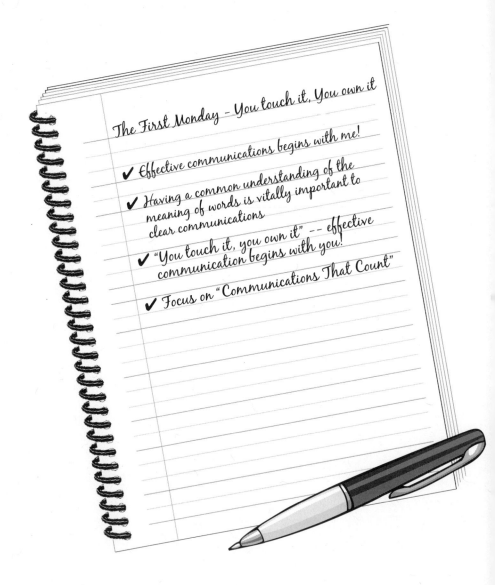

The First Monday – You touch it, You own it

✔ Effective communications begins with me!

✔ Having a common understanding of the meaning of words is vitally important to clear communications

✔ "You touch it, you own it" -- effective communication begins with you!

✔ Focus on "Communications That Count"

The Second Monday

Feedback: Breakfast
of Champions

*M*ichael looked a bit nervous as he joined me for our pre-meeting prior to driving to Tony's the following Monday. "I don't know about you, but Tony's simple little assignments turned out to be not so simple."

"I know what you mean. I've got most of his key points sorted out in my mind, but I will be surprised if I have all the answers."

Michael had worked out a grid of the *Communications That Count* he routinely encounters and I compared it to my own assessment. The biggest difference was in the mix of communications. I had a higher volume of e-mails, while Michael had more phone calls. But, we were both amazed at the sheer volume of communications we're involved in on a daily and weekly basis.

25

Here's Michael's chart:

Reporter's Questions	Involvement with *Communications That Count* (Weekly)					
Who	Inside: Team, Other Departments, Senior Management Outside: Suppliers, Channel Partners, Customers, Industry Association					
What	Project and program coordination, operations issues, pricing, employee relations, public relations… the gamut of business topics					
Where	Office, car, home, hotels, customer locations					
When	Could be 24/7 if I let it…					
How	E-Mail & IM	Phone & Voicemail	Meetings & Conference Calls	Intranet & Web	Faxes, memos & notes	Face-to-face
How Many (In & Out)	200	30	15	10	30	20
Why	Keep people informed, get things done, ask for support, etc.					

In the area of how effective we thought our communications were, we had both done a self-assessment and a quick survey with a sample group within our teams. As we talked, we developed a comparative table. Here's the rundown on Michael and his team:

Communications Method	Estimated Effectiveness (1-10)		
	Michael	Michael's Team	Gap
E-Mail & IM	6	5	-1
Phone & Voicemail	6	6	-
Meetings & Conference Calls	8	4	-4
Intranet & Web	7	5	-2
Faxes, Paper memos & notes	6	5	-1
Face-to-face	8	6	-2
Formal Presentations and Written Reports	6	5	-1
Overall	6	5	-1

"Wow!" said Michael. "When you look at the volume of communications we have going on and how ineffective some of them are, it's no wonder our teams are unhappy. These gaps, between what we perceive and what our teams perceive, are significant."

 It was 8:29:55 when we hit the porch and Tony swung the door open, just in time for us to be inside exactly at 8:30.

"Welcome back," Tony boomed, "I hope you're ready because I'm raring to go."

We looped through the kitchen and picked up coffee on our way to his study and then settled into the comfortable leather chairs.

"So how did the homework go?" Tony asked.

"It certainly was an eye-opener for me – for both of us," Michael said, "but I wound up with more questions than answers. I'm glad you're helping us work through it."

"Ditto," I said, "and frankly, I'm concerned about whether we can find a good fix, given the sheer volume of *Communications That Count* we touch every day. Even if I do a much better job – which I am bound and determined to do – we've got a big multiplier effect. With the number of people on our teams, we are sending and receiving hundreds of messages every day that need to be improved."

"Aha!" Tony said. "Now you understand why I'm always preaching about sharing what you learn. While you're both leaders, this isn't a problem you can fix by yourselves.

"So, let's take a look at your situation."

"Both Michael and I did a rundown independently," I explained, "but we put our heads together this morning and we've got a couple of tables that pretty well summarize our picture. However, Michael gets the credit for coming up with this analysis.".

"Thanks for the credit," Michael said, "and while my analysis isn't all that sophisticated, it does show what we're up against. We need solutions that will **radically** improve our mediocre effectiveness ratings, and close some big gaps between our views and the way our teams see things."

"Things sure have changed," Tony observed as Michael led him through the analysis. "E-mail volumes are way up but, at the same time, you actually may be enjoying some peace on the phone front.

"I can remember when I handled 50 to 60 calls a day," Tony continued, "but maybe 'peace' is the wrong word. Instant messaging is probably even more disruptive, especially if people you work with expect constant accessibility."

Tony put down the charts we had provided. "I'd like to go back to your analysis before we start talking about solutions, because I'm interested in what you think are the biggest issues and the major causes for your low effectiveness ratings.

"We talked a little last week about some of the causes of your communications problems, but did you get any new insights? Is it simply a volume problem? Or is it clarity or basic skills … or all of the above?"

"Actually, Tony, I really didn't take that deep of a dive," I admitted. "But to answer your question, I believe it's *all of the above*.

"My take is that we have a vicious cycle that begins with important messages poorly communicated. In turn, the lack of quality and clarity in these initial attempts create the need for more communications to clear things up. These added communication attempts contain their own errors and can introduce more confusion and emotional reactions that further complicate the situation.

"Last week we had an incident that illustrates this very problem. I've reconstructed what happened and made some notes:

E-mail from Dept Manager (DM) to Chris, cc Jeni: *I need the details on Smith right away.*
E-mail from Jeni to DM, cc Chris: *Chris is traveling this afternoon and I don't see anything about Smith on her desk. I did a computer search, though, and she has several Smiths within her files. I tried to reach you to find out which Smith, but had to leave a voice mail. I'm going to a meeting now, but will be back later and can research further.*
Voice mail from DM to Jeni: *Please look under Ronald B. Smith*
Voicemail from Jeni to DM: *No luck again – no Ronald B. Smith anywhere in plain sight and the account files under Smith on the computer are all different first names – no Ronald. I stopped by your office to talk with you about this, but now it appears you're gone for the day. Chris' airplane will be landing soon and I'll call her.*
Voicemail to Chris from Jeni on her cell phone line: *As soon as you land, please call the boss on his cell and fill him in on the Smsdsdf (garbled) matter. His number is 24 (garbled) 343 (garbled).*
Voicemail from Chris to DM on his cell: *I've been circling (garbled) for last three hours (garbled) you need something about the Schmidt situation, give me a buzz asdfk (garbled) I'll plug in my computer and send what you need. My number is 231 1 (garbled).*

Live phone call from Chris to DM (later that evening):

Chris: *I left you a message earlier, but didn't hear back so I thought I should call. I hope I'm not disturbing you and am sorry it took so long to connect, but how can I help you on the Schmidt matter?*

Boss: *(Angrily) Well, it's about time someone got back to me. I think you may have left a message earlier, but the name and number weren't clear. And by the way, it isn't Schmidt, it is Smith – you know, Ronnie Smith at Downtown Products and Services.*

Chris: *I'm so sorry about the delay. There was weather over Boston. Now to your inquiry– unfortunately, the Ronald B. Smith account was moved into Dave's area, I think to Pat, when we realigned last month. I can try to reach Dave or Pat at home if...*

Boss: *No, it's late and it's really not your problem. I'll get Jeni and Dave in my office in the morning and we'll work it out.*

"Of course, one case doesn't make a complete study, but this sort of thing happens way too often … and when it does, it's frustrating and it wastes time," I concluded. "On average, we're probably using four or more communications to do the job of one good one."

"I believe Jeni is 'right on,' " Michael said. "If we just got our messages straight the first time, we could move much faster because we wouldn't always be waiting for **the** answer."

"Bingo again," said Tony. "As in so many other businesses – and life – processes, getting it right the first time is an enormous positive. So later, we'll get into what it really takes to do it right the first time. But for now, I'm more interested in the other part of your homework assignment – your samples of effective communications and why you think they're good."

"I didn't have to look too far," Michael admitted. "My office is next door to the advertising department and they have what they call their inspirational wall. It's full of examples of things that have worked for other companies in the past. I could have brought fifty examples but picked one that also is a personal favorite.

"So ... the winner is the *got milk?* campaign from the American Dairy Farmers Association," Michael continued, obviously pleased with his selection. "This thing works on so many levels – visual, emotional, rational and subconscious – and has been effectively building business for the dairy folks for years. There's no doubt it is effective.

"Why does it work? There's a clear objective: get people to buy and drink more milk. The words are short, to the point, and ask for the order. People understand it and they remember it. Many of the ads with this theme include a humorous element, such as pictures of famous people with milk mustaches. Others play to powerful messages in our own memory that bring back vivid personal experiences.

"What would chocolate cake or brownies have been like without a tall glass of milk? Even if you couldn't choke down the beets or the broccoli, didn't your mom always say, 'Finish your milk'?"

"Great," said Tony. "I need to take a look at that wall one of these days. We can always learn a lot from the advertising world."

Reaching into the top drawer of his desk, he pulled out a well worn scrap of paper. "Years ago, an account exec from an ad agency gave me this quotation and I think it speaks volumes in just a few words.

> **David Belasco, the great American theatrical producer once said,**
>
> *"If you can't write your idea on the back of my calling card, you don't have a clear idea."*

"That's good … really good," I said. "When I was looking for my example, I looked at advertising and entertainment also. Then, I took a look at some famous communications from public figures – trying to find something short and to the point that delivered a complex message. The Martin Luther King 'I have a dream' speech has some serious horsepower, as did Franklin D. Roosevelt's 'A date that will live in infamy' speech. But the example I finally picked includes just six words Ronald Reagan spoke at the Brandenburg Gate in West Berlin on June 12, 1987:

Mr. Gorbachev, tear down this wall!

"Strong words, right? But in communications, the proof is in the results. Reagan *achieved the objectives* outlined in his speech and, within two years, got the Soviets to take action.

"Those six words brought down the wall. The Brandenburg Gate reopened in 1989 for the first time in 40 years, and the two Germanys reunited in 1990.

"That's a great example," Tony said, "and moves us to our next point. At the core of the communications process is first defining, and then achieving, a *clear objective*. If you don't know what you want to accomplish, you're going to waste a lot of time and words talking around a topic. You won't get anything done and may wind up sending a message that actually *creates* confusion.

"So, I want to be clear about what I mean when I talk about objectives," Tony said. "Never hurts to practice what you preach."

"Clear *Objectives* can be captured in short sentences that begin with an action word and define what you want to accomplish.

"*Specific Desired Outcomes* are building blocks that add up to an objective. These are described in short phrases or sentences that begin with an action word and describe the changes in attitudes or actions you need.

"Another way to look at this is to think of *objectives as motives* – the 'whys' behind our words and deeds.

"On television, the homicide detectives are always interested in finding **the** *motive* to help sort out the real perpetrator from the rest of the suspects. When there's no apparent motive, it's either a *senseless crime* committed by a person that needs to be committed or one where the detectives have to go back and dig deeper.

"To get closure, they need to find a plausible objective – the real driver of the vicious action – to lead them to the actual perpetrator.

"In some ways, bad communications are a lot like senseless crimes – they are *crimes without motives*. Without a clear objective, we're left to try to figure out what the sender is trying to say or accomplish," Tony concluded, stopping to take a sip of coffee.

"Okay. For next week, I would like for you to think about how you can improve the clarity of objectives for your own communications," Tony said, settling back in his chair. Then, I'd like you to focus on the things that need fixing to make your communications work the first time.

"Finally, I'd also like to see your action plan about how you're going to tackle the overall problem."

Pausing briefly to reflect, Tony continued. "I think we've covered a lot of ground today, and I hope you aren't on total overload at this point."

"Well," I began slowly, "I am going to need a little time for all of this to soak in."

"And we've really just begun," Michael pointed out.

"Yes," Tony agreed. "This matter of communications can be a very complicated business, so we will want to stick to the fundamentals to avoid getting way off track.

"To make that happen, I suggest you make your own notes on what we talked about, and then put your notebook aside for a day or two before coming back to it ... and be sure you get a good night's sleep next Sunday!"

Later that day, I posted my notes into my Monday Morning notebook:

2nd Monday with Tony

✔ Communicating can be a vicious cycle Higher volumes are driven by poor quality and ineffective initial communications that in turn, trigger more ineffective repeat attempts

✔ Short and concise is better than long and complicated

✔ Vivid images – visual graphics and mental pictures are major elements of effective communications (e.g. "got milk" campaign)

✔ Choose strong words!

✔ A clear objective is a critical foundation

The Third Monday
Communications Triage

"GOOD MORNING JENI!" Michael was almost shouting as we met in the parking lot. "I figure if I speak louder it will make my weak case a bit stronger!" "I know what you mean," I said, taking a folder out of my briefcase. "I've used that approach and the opposite trick – speaking very softly – to get people to lean in and listen, even when they don't want to hear what I have to say. Either way, I don't think Tony will be buying any tricks, so what have we got?"

"Here's what I put together for the part about of objectives," Michael said sheepishly. "It's a pretty simple-minded device I call a MLH (Michael's Little Helper), but it seems to work. I taped it to my computer monitor and my last 20 to 30 e-mails have been much better. Take a look:

Michael's MLH on Communications Objectives	
What	What *exactly* do I want to happen as a result of this note?
Who	Who needs to do something? Who needs to know about it and/or cares if it gets done? Who has needed information?
When	When does this need to happen? Are there interim deadlines? What are the consequences of not making the timing?
Why	Why do I want this to happen? What's in it for me and for others – why should they want to help? What are objections?
How	Are specific methods needed or can we focus more on results than process? Is cost a factor? Which quality standards apply?

"Pretty slick," I agreed, "and you can bet I'll have a copy on my monitor before lunch."

Michael laughed, "Only after we get Tony's blessing. If he doesn't like it, I may need to disown it."

 Tony was waiting for us, as usual, as we arrived with a minute or two to spare.

"Are your minds still scrambled or did the rest period I prescribed work?"

"It was just what the doctor ordered," I said as we bounded up the steps with an extra spring in our walk.

"Swell," said Tony. "I'm ready to go as well."

We grabbed our customary coffee and settled in. Michael began

38

our meeting with his "Michael's Little Helper," which immediately earned Tony's enthusiastic approval.

"This is fantastic," he said, "and I know exactly where I'm going to tape up my copy. Even the best communicators get writer's block once in a while, and when we're rushed, we all have a tendency to be a little careless. This will definitely help."

"Okay", I said, "it's my turn for show and tell. I fell a little behind on my homework this weekend because I wound up spending most of yesterday afternoon in the Emergency Room. My seven-year-old fell out of a tree and wound up with a sprained arm. He's fine – no cast was needed – but I wanted to share what I learned quite unexpectedly.

"As I sat in the ER waiting room, I had a good opportunity to observe their triage process, and I believe it teaches us something about solving our communications problems."

"What's medicine got to do with communications?" Michael asked, as Tony listened intently.

"Well here's the parallel. The triage process prioritizes the needs of people coming into the emergency room so they are treated in order of the severity of their problems. The process also assures that incoming patients are routed to the proper specialists needed to treat their conditions.

"Using triage prevents errors such as treating someone with the sniffles ahead of someone bleeding profusely. It also assures that people who may have broken bones get sent for X-rays as soon as possible.

"I hadn't thought of the triage analogy," Tony admitted, "but I think it works, not only here on communications problems but also on other business issues, too. If we forget to stop the bleeding first, the corrective actions that follow aren't likely to do much good."

"I hadn't thought of it either," Michael added, "but it's pretty clear we have a little triage work to do ourselves. We really need to sort out our issues by severity and by the kind of fixes that may be needed."

"Exactly," Tony agreed. "Have you come up with any categories to use to do your analysis?"

"I took our survey data and looked for the underlying problems we need to address," I said. "Here are the five big issues I've identified:

- ♦ **Purpose & Logic** – this includes clarity of objectives and desired outcomes, "what's in it for me" considerations and logic flow.

- ♦ **Media Selection** is a big one – we need to make better choices when it comes to e-mail vs. phone vs. face-to-face, etc.

- ♦ **Construction** – these are basic skills matters – grammar and syntax, spelling and punctuation and other elements that add up to clear and concise messages.

- ♦ **Tone & Style** – this is where we look at things like use of humor, an emotional or logical approach, etc.

- ♦ **Credibility & Trust** – this includes authenticity, honesty, candor/openness, data, evidence, corroboration, proof – all the elements needed to have and deliver the straight story.

"Unfortunately, all of these seem to be in the critical 'stop the bleeding' category," I concluded.

"Let's think about this a minute," Tony suggested. "All these matters are important building blocks for good communications, but do **all** of your people have **all** of these problems? Do **all** of your weak communications exhibit **all** of these faults? And more importantly, what's behind these faults – is it a lack of knowledge or skill or could it be it be something more benign, like time pressure or fatigue?

"No," I said, breathing a small sigh of relief, "I don't think everyone has every problem."

"But," Michael said, "if this is the list we're working on, it still looks like a pretty big job. It doesn't look like we can use the old 'eat the elephant one bite at a time' approach.

"Even though everyone doesn't have all of the problems, the whole thing needs to be fixed – and fast. It looks like it could be a major undertaking and we're already seriously overloaded..."

"Hold on," Tony interrupted. "Couldn't you use the 'divide and conquer' approach to cut the workload part of this down to size?"

Tony's question was followed by two highly audible sighs of relief. Clearly, a big chunk of our problem wasn't related to the basic skills of our people but, rather, to their present situation. We were not, in fact, against the wall we imagined because here was Tony, pointing the way out of our dilemma.

"So, we can cut down the workload considerably and spread it out, as in 'many hands make light work,'" said Michael. So, for starters, I know Kim in HR would be willing to work on this. Then, we've got access to a real expert in you, Tony, for a few more weeks. Plus, I've got some budget I can use for formal training."

"I have some money left in my training budget as well," I said, "and we have some excellent people on our teams who can help. On the expertise front, Michael, don't sell yourself short. You may not have majored in English, but you're well known as one of the best troubleshooters in the company."

"Okay," Michael said. "I'm now both relieved and convinced we can work our way through this.

"Speaking of troubleshooting, let's move to the third part of our homework," said Tony, maneuvering us back on task. "Here's a simple model for problem-solving I've used in the past."

Three-Step Problem Solving

1. Frame the Issue and Get Facts
2. Understand Data and Clarify Problems
3. Develop Solutions and Action Plans

"This is great," I said, "and I believe the basic survey, our follow-up work on effectiveness perceptions and my categories for the analysis all fit into this model. It looks to me like we're well into Step 2."

"I agree with Jeni," Michael said. "I believe our next step is to run the triage process to prioritize our issues and pick ones we're going to take on. We're not ready to move to solutions yet, but it won't take long.

"I think we can obtain the information we need to complete the triage process by conducting some focus groups," I offered. "If we were to trade groups – I facilitate a focus group with Michael's team and he does one with mine – we might be able to get more candid answers. This could be especially helpful if our employees believe their managers are causing some of these concerns.

"Our main objective with these groups would be to find the areas of greatest need and prioritize where to go first."

But before I could finish, Tony interrupted me. "A point I need to raise here," Tony continued, "is something you'll figure out on your own later, but I'll save you a little heartburn between now and when you get the 'aha!'

"Triage, whether it's in an ER or in your work situation, is rarely linear," he said. "You'll have to take on many of these problems simultaneously, exactly the same way the emergency room deals with the cases they see. Keeping a shock victim warm involves blankets – not neurosurgeons. In your situation, you don't want all of your patients queued up for surgery when all they need is a penicillin injection."

"Brilliant analogy, Tony," I said, "but I'm disappointed that I didn't think of it!"

Tony, as usual, modestly accepted the compliment. "Being the consultant is sometimes the easy job because I don't share your pain and I have enough distance to see a larger picture. But without your exploratory work, I wouldn't have been able to put two and two together. So let's move on. Tell me about your next steps in getting this thing kicked off."

"I thought maybe we could brainstorm a few ideas right now," Michael responded. "Jeni and I can buff them up later today and then develop a completed plan for you to see next week."

"Good idea," said Tony, "so to get us started, let me share a few tips I learned long ago. First off, I think it's important for you to write down and publicly announce what you're planning to your teams. This will not only firm up your personal commitment to the project, but more importantly, it promises your people that you are moving quickly on something that's important to them."

"We probably should ask Kim to join us in this announcement because I'm almost certain we'll be eventually talking about some formal skill-building training," I said, thinking out loud. "Of course, we'll be funding this, but she will arrange the program for us."

"Right," Michael said, "and we may also need HR support to do some individual interviews if we have people who prefer to give their input confidentially. "

"Good idea. As soon as I get back to the office, I'll schedule a meeting with Kim," I offered.

Tony was next to speak. "So, will you announce this to your teams via an e-mail, staff meetings or what?"

"We want to get the word out quickly – as soon as we have the plans firmed up and have Kim on board," Michael said. "So, I think a brief, all-hands meeting later this week would be a good way to do it. We can do our focus groups immediately following the all-hands while people have the overall picture fresh in their minds."

"I agree," I said, "and the face-to-face lets us handle questions and solicit volunteers to work on the project. We'll back this up with an e-mail and intranet posting to make sure we cover people who are out of the office.

"Looking ahead, we won't be able to have a meeting at every step of the way but we'll use the electronic media to keep everyone informed."

"Okay," said Tony. "You have your homework for next week – a recap of the total plan. My commitment to you for next week is to help you make it as good a plan as the three of us can invent!

"And, once again," Tony said, "our little trio got a lot done this morning. See you next week!"

As we walked to our cars, Michael remarked, "Well there's no turning back now, and while I'm still not sure how I can juggle all I have going on, I couldn't expect to accomplish nearly as much if I were working on this alone."

"You're absolutely right, Michael, and I have a good feeling about the time we're investing – we might actually find ourselves going home earlier after we complete this project."

Later, I entered the highlights from the session in my notebook:

3rd Monday with Tony

✔ Use the Reporter's Questions (Who, What, When, Why...) to help shape your objectives and desired outcomes

✔ Communications is a complex topic with several potential trouble spots:
- Purpose & Logic
- Media Selection
- Mechanical & Rational
- Tone & Style
- Credibility & Trust

✔ Identify and prioritize corrective actions needed using a "triage" process

✔ Team approach to solution will spread workload and improve buy-in

The Fourth Monday
Turning Unknowns into Knowns

M ichael was leaning against his car when I arrived at Tony's the next Monday, looking sharp and composed even after a family emergency involving spilled milk had cancelled our pre-meeting.

Quick recovery I thought, and took a risk on setting him off again by saying, "Got milk?" Michael chuckled as we walked up the drive.

 Tony greeted us with his usual warmth, and then surprised us with some new personalized coffee cups when we stopped in the kitchen. "Take a look at these," he said. "They're prototypes for ones I'm going to order for an executive conference next month. I'm big on little things like this – it's a low key way to bring people into the family, so to speak."

"I hadn't really thought about mementos," I remarked, "but you're right. I have a pretty sizable collection of personalized t-shirts, hats and coffee cups, myself. I can tell you exactly when and where I received every one of them … and I'm still in touch with people I've worked with on past team-building and community service projects."

"Me too," added Michael, "I'm not big on memorabilia in general, but the ones with my name on them have pretty good staying power."

We settled in for the morning's work and Tony suggested we start with the action plan that Michael and I had worked out in some detail the prior week.

"How about if I take you through this, Tony," I offered, "and then you can give us your reactions?"

"Perfect. Let's get started," Tony nodded.

Communications That Count Action Plan

When (Week #)	What (Planned Actions)	Why (Connection to Objectives Outcomes)
1	Announcement & Focus Group Meetings	Build program awareness & understand problems.
2	Triage	ID Top Ten Issues and quick fixes ("just do its") and "hot potato" needs for individual counseling.
3	Quick Fix Roll-out and coaching. Plan Top 10 actions.	Move fast on obvious problems. Coordination with others will be needed on Top 10.
4	Progress Meeting	Explain Top 10 plans to assure everyone participates and feels good about it.
4-6	Execute Top 10 improvements	Time needed to conduct training and self-development work.
7	Conduct Evaluation Survey and Analyze Findings	Did it work? Can we declare victory and move on or are other actions needed?
8	Program Conclusion Meeting & Documentation	Review results with teams and thank them for their participation and support. Capture key findings for future use by others.

"Well, it's pretty clear you've had some experience in action planning because I really don't have much to add," Tony said as I concluded ... "but I do have a question for you. This is going to be a fairly long undertaking because you'll have to have some training and other actions that can't be accomplished immediately – so how are you going to keep the momentum going?"

"We didn't put it on this action plan," Michael replied, "but Kim, Jeni and I will be touching base every week in a brief meeting or conference call. This will be important during the implementation as some tasks will be done by other individuals.

49

"Another item we didn't list in the plan – we're also going to meet with our bosses before we kick this thing off," I explained. "While we can handle the actions needed, they should be in the loop every step of the way."

"Once again, you've covered all the bases," said Tony, "as I'm coming to expect. At the same time, I think we need to back up to the bigger picture for a moment.

"What you've put together, so far, is very good," Tony began, "and I don't have issues with any of your ideas individually. Somehow though, when you add up all of the rules and guidelines you'll likely have when you're done, the whole thing has sort of a …"

"… starchy feel?" I suggested.

"Exactly," said Tony. "It could wind up coming off like the lectures our mothers used to give about sitting up straight and eating our vegetables.

"All the rules and suggestions you'll lay out are important, and 'right' in isolation … but what we really want to achieve is for communications to be **more effective**. We want e-mails and memos that are clear and purposeful, not sonnets that will win poetry awards.

"So, we need to figure out how you can frame the ideas and present them so that your people aren't really put off by all of these rules."

Michael and I nodded our agreement.

"Let's take a break and mull this around in our heads while we reload our coffee cups," Tony suggested. "Maybe we'll come back with an inspiration...."

"By Jove!" Tony said as he returned to the library, "I've got it! I have a distant cousin on my father's great uncle's side of the family, and he may have the framework for the solution we need.

"Here's a piece of trivia. Their forefathers arrived at Ellis Island at a different time, so they spell their name P-I-E-R-C-E and we spell it P-E-A-R-C-E – but well, that's another story.

"In any event, my cousin – Benjamin Franklin Pierce – had a way of describing what he did that fits almost exactly what we're trying to do here. You may have heard of him. On TV, he went by the nickname Hawkeye, which he picked up from his favorite book, *The Last of the Mohicans.*

"Yes, I know this storytelling makes me sound a bit like I'm stalling, but it gives me time to get my thoughts together. What I'm talking about is the concept of 'meatball surgery' on the M*A*S*H television program – you have seen it, haven't you – even though it probably first aired before you were born?"

After we assured Tony there probably wasn't an adult on the planet that hadn't seen at least one M*A*S*H episode, he went on.

"In those wartime surgical units close to the front, the staff often faced an overwhelming volume of very serious cases. They practiced what Hawkeye called 'meatball surgery' because it wasn't always neat and rarely pretty.

"They were in the business of saving lives, and in the extra time it would take to make a procedure textbook-perfect instead of perfectly functional, another patient could die.

"Now Hawkeye and his peers were not careless, but they developed this special skill – to be both good **and** fast – literally in the heat of battle.

"To be fully functional in the war zone, they needed to quickly build the skills and confidence to get it *right enough the first time* while keeping their eye on the ball – saving as many lives as they could.

"Your job, in the rapid-paced world you live in, is much the same. Maybe your objective isn't literally saving lives – but it's important to your company's bottom line and, potentially, to your company's survival over time.

"So here's the idea," Tony continued. "You need to sell your teams on the idea that communications must improve, but they also need to know that *perfection is not the goal.*

"You need to make this point clear: there is a *need for speed* built into your goals and greater *effectiveness* is the target. But speed doesn't mean making mistakes big enough to cause your communications to fail, as they often do now.

"Bottom line, adopt the 'meatball surgery' mindset to get your messages *right enough the first time.*

"Tony," I said, "this is simply brilliant! I'll have to admit, I was worried I was going to come off like the school teacher who rapped the backs of kids' hands with rulers."

"I had that same feeling," Michael added, "but I hadn't yet figured out what was causing it. Your concept, as I used to say, is 'awesome, dude'! So, how do we put it into our plan?"

"Ah," Tony said, "as you know, timing can be everything, so I think you probably should hold this thought until you roll out the whole plan. At that point, people will be delighted to hear that your plan doesn't include the 'grammar police.'"

"Good idea," Michael said. "As you saw in our timetable, we have a meeting planned about a month from now to reveal the whole program."

"We can talk more about it later, but you may want to think ahead about using a theme for that meeting to help promote the 'right enough the first time' concept," Tony suggested.

"But, before we run out of time, let's shift gears and focus on some specific types of *Communications That Count* that are particularly important to you as managers and leaders – meetings and presentations.

"So we don't stack 'make work' on top of the real stuff, for next Monday I'd like you to bring me materials you will use in the kick-off meetings you've scheduled.

"A few years ago, a friend of mine gave me a job aid for preparing meetings and presentations, and I think you'll find it helpful," Tony continued. "You're already using the *Reporter's Questions*, and this device uses them to organize presentations and meetings.

"Based on my experience, it really works to reduce stress and lets you move forward faster. The idea is to 'turn unknowns into knowns.' Like your 'Michael's Little Helper' helps develop objectives, this provides a simple way to get ready for an important session," Tony explained.

"It's pretty basic and I can sketch it for you now. You start with a name for the event that implies its purpose. Then, you define the objective(s) and desired outcomes for the session.

Meeting Subject/Purpose:
Overall Objective(s):
Desired Outcomes:

"Next, look at stakeholders and participants whose needs you must address. This, by the way, is a really important step. If you don't know your audience and you don't know what others are expecting, you're headed for trouble," our mentor cautioned. "For example, I'll bet the Controller will ask how you're going to pay for this and someone is going to ask how you plan to offset the workload. There's also a place to note any unique timing or scheduling considerations.

Key Stakeholders
Meeting Participants
Timing/Scheduling:

"With that information listed, you're ready to design the content and flow. You use the 'why' column exactly as you did in your action plan to assure each element contributes to your overall objective and desired outcomes. The 'how' column is where you note your method of delivery and visual aids.

#	Time	Who	What	Why	How

"Finally, this tool helps you think ahead about information that may be required and arrangements that need to be handled before the event:

Pre-work and/or Key Information Required:
Room Layout:
Facilities, Equipment Required:
Documentation Plan (need Recorder/Scribe?):
Ground Rules:

"This is great, Tony," I said. "Much better than the worksheet I normally use – uh, er, when I use one...."

"Well, I've learned the hard way about why I should always use this," Tony said, "after bombing a couple of times in meetings and presentations I foolishly thought were gimmies. The same guy I got this tool from drew me a simple picture about how preparation fits into what it takes to be highly effective.

"He says the 'iceberg principle' applies directly to highly effective communications – and I agree – especially the important meetings and presentations we're talking about right now.

"What people can't see – your preparation – is as important as the delivery they can see. Without both at professional levels, you won't get what you want.

"Think of your meeting or presentation as a ship. If you haven't done your homework, you are at risk of running into something you haven't anticipated. This lack of preparation will frequently sink your ship," Tony explained.

"On the positive side, though, people who pay attention to both preparedness and delivery are more consistently effective and earn big bonuses in terms of credibility, acceptance and success."

Tony took a moment to finish his coffee. "I have a lot more thoughts in this area, but we'll have to come back to those later because we're about out of time," he said, "but before you go, I want you to know how proud I am of what our team has accomplished today."

*   *   *

I added this to my notebook later in the day:

The Fifth Monday

Go Slow to
Go Fast

The next Monday was a clear and beautiful day.

"Glad to see you're a bit early," Tony said, meeting us at the door. "I know you have important things planned for this week and I want to hear all about them!"

"You're right," I said. "We have a lot going this week that fits the definition of *Communications That* **Really** *Count.*

"But before we begin reviewing what's coming up, I wanted to mention that our meetings with HR and our bosses went extremely well. Everyone's on board with what we want to do and how we plan to go about it.

"Going forward, we'll keep them briefed and they'll be there if we need them," I added.

It was Michael's turn next. "Okay, here are our Meeting Preparation Worksheets for the Launch Meeting and the Focus Group," he began. "As promised, your framework was easy to use and helped us design the sessions easily.

"Next, Jeni will take you through the launch meeting agenda to give you a sense of what we're planning, minus the details," Michael continued, "but I need to add a footnote first.

"Jeni and I were both struck with the realization we have an enormous opportunity to back our words with deeds, and face a major risk if we don't. If we're serious about improving communications, then we must be committed do the best we can in the process.

"As we learned last week, we don't have to be perfect," Michael pointed out, "but we absolutely positively need to show we're giving this project our best efforts and need to be 'right enough' to get the job done the first time."

"A little 'fear factor,' huh?" Tony inquired. "Well, this is the kind of fear that I promote. Fear is sort of like cholesterol," he explained. "There are good and bad types. This good type of fear shows to me – and will demonstrate to your teams – you are recognizing your responsibilities as leaders. Properly harnessed, this kind of fear can drive you toward great accomplishments!"

"I suppose you're right," I said. "In fact I know you're right, but getting those little butterflies in my stomach hitched up to pull the wagon isn't easy."

"You're right," Tony agreed, "but it gets easier once you learn to recognize the kind of fear you're facing and get some practice turning unknowns into knowns."

"To give you a better idea of what we're planning, here's the agenda we'll be using for the Launch Meeting," I said, handing a copy to Tony:

Agenda		
Meeting Subject	Launch *Communications That Count* Program	
Overall Objective	Inform Teams about plans to correct Communications issues	
TIME **WHO**		**WHAT**
10:00 Jeni & Michael		• Opening Comments and Introductions • Review Ground Rules, Desired Outcomes & Agenda
10:10 Michael		• Survey results & importance of corrective actions • Collaborative approach – two teams with support from HR
10:20 Jeni		• High Level Program structure and timetable • Near-term actions – Focus Groups • Solution Development • Implementation
10:30 Kim		• Importance of active participation by all • Michael & Jeni will facilitate focus groups for opposite teams • Need candid inputs – HR is available for issues you don't want to share in an open session
10:40 All		• Open Q&A
10:50 Jeni & Michael		• Recap • Distribute Meeting Evaluation Forms and Adjourn
Ground Rules		
1) Cellular Phones and PDAs off. Pagers muted. 2) We plan to stick to the agenda in terms of content and timing. 3) Interesting, but off-agenda items will be placed in the Parking Lot for disposition near the end of the meeting if time permits or to be handled off-line later. 4) Passionate Participation is encouraged. Personal attacks are not. Please wear your "corporate hat."		

"I'm happy to see you don't plan to close with the Q&A," Tony observed. "It took me a while to learn this, but it's really smart to move it up a little. All you need is one loose cannon with a negative comment or inappropriate question and you'll have an otherwise good meeting ruined … that is, **if** you don't have a separate recap agenda item to refocus attention back on the positives."

"And in line with your 'loose cannon' comment, we did work through some 'what if' scenarios," Michael explained. "Some people have difficulty separating their issues, and will be tempted to wander off into other matters on the Employee Survey, like overtime schedules and compensation plan matters. We need to be ready if people bend our ground rules."

"Now that you mention your ground rules," Tony remarked, "I see you've covered an item that's a growing pet peeve for me. People who think they can meet with me and do their e-mail at the same time just boggle my mind. They think they're being super-efficient by multi-tasking but, instead, they're running at half-speed because they aren't doing either very well.

"Don't get me wrong – I'm not anti-electronics. I use a hand-held device for wireless access to e-mail when I'm traveling or while waiting for meetings to start. However, I wouldn't *think* of disrespecting someone by clicking away on my handheld while they were talking to me."

"Not to change the subject, but what do you think of our meeting plan?" Michael wanted to know.

"Once again, I'm almost speechless because I have little to add, but

I do have an observation. I'm pretty sure you've had some good training about meeting design somewhere along the way because my little form doesn't fill itself out," Tony observed with a wry grin.

"You're right," Michael confessed. "We both attended a training program on effective meetings a couple of years ago, but have been backsliders until this one came up. In fact, we're pretty sure this kind of training will come out as a major need on the early 'just do it' list, and your job aid will be offered in our packets."

"Talking about your 'just do it' list Tony said, "I know you plan to use focus groups to develop a 'top ten' list your teams will buy into, but it might be helpful to identify some of the actions now.

"If you go into your focus groups with a draft list, it may be easier to get to the ten you want. Of course, you'll want to enter fairly softly and then listen carefully. I often use what I call the 'Colombo' routine. This is a very humble approach.

"You make it clear you may not have the picture *exactly* right, but you do have some clues. Colombo would say something like 'Ma'am, there are just a few things I need to clear up, but it seems to me ....'

"That's a great approach," Michael agreed. "To get the list started, I'm sure we'll want to put some training in business writing on the list ... and maybe a little guidance about how to use the Reporter's Questions to frame objectives for all kinds of *Communications That Count ....*"

"Great ideas," Tony said, pulling his flip chart stand into our circle and grabbing a pad of large yellow stickies. "Let's write these down ... and what else can we think of as a 'just do it'?"

"Based on our own experience, we'll need to do follow-up to assure people stick with what they learn in the training," I suggested.

"Those all sound good to me," Michael said, "and how about this? We all really need to take more care in developing our communications. We've gotten sloppy because there's never enough time, but if we were to just slow down and pay attention to what we're trying to say, our communications wouldn't be such a mess.

"Maybe setting down some guidelines would be a gentle reminder about the things to avoid like:

- ◆ Lack of key facts or data and one-sided stories
- ◆ Typos, punctuation, grammar and syntax errors that lead to confusion
- ◆ Meaning of words not made clear and acronyms not spelled out at first usage

"Guidelines on these areas are a good idea," Tony said, "but what about the '*thinko*?' "

I broke the silence. "Well, my vocabulary is pretty good, but I don't think I've ever heard of 'thinko' before."

"Aha! I've finally found a word that stumps the straight-A students," Tony joked. "A thinko is much like a typo, but relates to logic or factual errors in a message. The usual cause is rushing or fatigue, but sometimes it's just plain not thinking a matter through."

"I get it," Michael spoke up. "My pet name for that kind of error is *synapse lapse*, but I like 'thinko' better."

"Call them anything you want," Tony said, "but it's too bad Bill Gates hasn't come up with a *Thinko Finder* to go along with the Spell Check function."

"And it's too bad some people are in such a hurry that they don't bother to use spell check," Michael added, "because when you get a few good typos coupled with one thinko and a grammatical error or three, you wind up with a puzzle most people won't take the time to solve."

That reminded Tony of an old saying popularized by Jackie Stewart, the three-time world driving champion. "Jackie says, 'go slow to go fast,' and after you let it soak in a minute, it makes real sense.

"If you roar at full throttle onto a new track, the likely outcome is not a fast lap but a crash. Jackie's approach is to go slowly at first, learn the track and work your way up to record-setting lap times."

"*Go slow to go fast* – that sounds like a great headline for our guidelines," I said. "Let's put it on the flipchart."

"So what else do you have in the 'obvious action' category?" Tony wanted to know. "What about picking the right medium for your messages?"

"More content for our guidelines," I said. "It may be pretty obvious, but we all rush too much and sometimes pick the wrong conduits."

"Yes," Tony agreed. "Even people willing to solve puzzles get annoyed or frustrated with the way some people *choose to communicate.*"

"There are plenty of examples of this," I continued. "If you take a scenario where you and I want to set up a lunch meeting, you can paint a pretty good picture of this problem. Using e-mail, it could take six individual messages to negotiate a date, time and place for a get together, while a single phone call could get it done."

"Yes indeed," Tony agreed, "and I'll bet you'll also hear one of my favorites in this category that is way more serious – it's the one I call the *egregious electronic performance review* – where someone with limited tact decides to chew out another via e-mail instead of face-to-face. When the facts aren't quite right or the conclusions are contentious, these little gems can start raging wars!"

"Well, without too much effort, we've generated a pretty sizable number of concerns we can act on pretty quickly," I pointed out.

"At the same time, remember you're working on communications problems from your teams' perspectives. And while you're in range, you may not have these absolutely nailed," Tony reminded.

We nodded and he went on. "So I think it could be fruitful if you would just carry these as 'tentative' for the moment."

Here's what our tentative list looked like:

Communications That Count
Tentative "Just Do It" List

➤ Training
- Business writing
- Effective meetings

➤ "Go Slow to Go Fast" Guidelines
- Use the Reporter's Questions
- Get facts or data to build a complete story
- Use care to avoid typos, thinkos and grammatical errors
- Define terms and acronyms

➤ Pick best medium
- Phone or face-to-face when interaction or immediate resolution is important
- Meetings or conference calls when interaction is needed and more people are involved
- E-mail works well in a wide variety of situations, but not for sensitive matters or emotional interchanges

---

"On the homework front" Tony said, "you'll be having your kickoff meeting and your focus groups on Wednesday, right? So how about bringing in a revised action plan next Monday?" Michael acknowledged the assignment with a perfect Colombo impression as we got up to leave. Tony cracked up and we laughed our way to the door … another very successful session concluded with a smile.

Later, I put a copy of the flip chart content in my Monday Morning notebook, along with my notes. My entry looked like this:

5th Monday with Tony

✔ Harness the "fear factor" to be as good as we can be

✔ Good meeting plan, but don't skip rehearsals

✔ Must back our words with deeds during project

✔ Assure that candidates identified for "just do it's," address team issues.

✔ Use the "Colombo" routine to enter softly and then listen carefully

✔ Go Slow To Go Fast

The Sixth Monday
Do No Harm

*I*t was raining cats and dogs the next Monday, but just as we pulled into Tony's driveway, the rain subsided and the sun emerged through the clouds. It was going to be a beautiful day.

"Good morning," smiled Tony as he opened the door. "Don't you just love the smell of the air just after a rain?"

 After collecting our coffee and making our way to our now familiar seats in Tony's library, I led off with some observations about our launch meetings.

"You were right to push us on our preparation for the launch meetings Tony," I began. "We received high marks and really positive feedback from our teams and upper management. In retrospect, planning seems like such a simple step, we really can't afford to have meetings without a thorough prep. It more than paid back the effort we put into it in terms of effectiveness and employee satisfaction, and it definitely reduced our stress levels going in."

"Isn't it amazing what taking the unknowns and turning them into knowns can do for you?" Tony remarked. "But, were there any surprises?"

"Only pleasant ones, Tony," Michael chimed in. "We had people from my team who usually sit through meetings without making a peep asking really good questions."

"And one of my team members who is usually a real sourpuss took the time to see me afterwards, pointing out this work is really needed and that Michael and I are the right ones to lead it," I added.

"The indirect feedback from the 'meetings after the launch meeting' was positive as well," Michael added, "and the focus groups went exactly the same way, with good evaluations and positive individual comments.

"The idea to have us facilitate each other's group worked extremely well because I'm pretty sure we heard, candidly, from at least a few people who might not have opened up in front of the person who writes their performance reviews."

"Great," said Tony, "or as Dr. W. Edwards Deming, the famous Quality Control expert, would say, 'It's exactly as I expected it would be.' You put the quality into your plan and then worked your plan.

"So, what did you learn? You went in with a good 'just do it' list we built last week, but I'll bet you picked up quite a few more. What are the new biggies on your *Communications That Count* action list?"

"First of all, our list from last week survived pretty much intact," I began. "We got a lot more examples and more details about various points, but we were on the right track with those items we came up with beforehand.

"We also picked up concerns in several other categories we can address with fast actions and we learned, too, about needs in areas that we probably won't be covering directly in our near-term action plans. At the same time, we can't ignore these concerns altogether and would like your thoughts on what we might do with some of them.

"As far as what we've learned, we've grouped the results from the focus groups into several categories. For each category, we have a few descriptive comments along with our thoughts about what may be needed to correct the issues. Next is a column with our ideas for things we can do right away to get the early successes we need.

"We won't drag you through all of the detail we have on these," I promised, "but suffice it to say we have enough data to develop solutions.

"Now, let's take a look at the first group of issues we've bundled under the category called *Sheer Volume*. What we heard about here is a real issue, at the gut level. There are **just too many** e-mails and instant messages.

"We think some of the items on our 'just do it' list from last week will help, and we got some good suggestions on spam filters and etiquette guides that will make a difference. As an example, one simple etiquette item that can whack hundreds of e-mails out of our system is to stop the extra e-mails that only say 'thank you' and 'you're welcome.'"

"Jeni and I believe we also need to start tracking volumes and really pay attention to absolute numbers until we get this under control," Michael said. At a minimum, we need to have data to consider follow-up action if it seems needed."

"I see" said Tony. "None of this is surprising, but I'm pleased to see you plan to do some measurements. It will be interesting to see what people on your teams think of as 'too many.' I also believe that 'too many' may really be a disguised version of 'too many **unclear** messages,' which isn't a volume matter at all. Your guidelines and etiquette tips will certainly help in that regard."

"It also may mean too many **emotional** messages, as well," Michael reported. "Some of our folks put up with a fair volume of notes from people with apparently no sensitivity at all. We heard stories about long-running 'gun battles' ...."

"Just like the Hatfields and the McCoys," I interjected. "One of my people brought in a string of e-mails that read like *War and Peace*, except peace had yet to arrive."

"Well," said Tony, "this is one area where your guidelines alone won't get the job done. You may want to do some fairly simple interpersonal skills training on how to call truces peer-to-peer, and how to establish and maintain peace treaties.

"You could teach the basics in a staff meeting in no more than 15 minutes. Of course, you may have to directly intervene in the worst cases, but it would be better if people learn how to gracefully settle their own disputes or at least be civil in their communications.

"Even if I'm really upset with you for some reason, it doesn't have to be front and center in the e-mails I send. Business communications need to be businesslike ... period."

"I'll add it to the list," I said, retrieving the flip chart and starting a new page.

"Next," said Michael, "is a topic that didn't surprise us and won't surprise you either. But it brought up details that were both interesting and actionable. It appears there are not only meeting management problems – which we'll work on with training – but also some mechanical items training can't fix.

"As supervisors, Jeni and I don't have problems finding meeting space, but we've now learned this is not the case for the troops. Bottom line, we have to fix our conference room reservation system and make sure our rooms are kept ready to go. We need to assure they are supplied with flip charts and markers and all equipment is in good working order."

"You're right," said Tony. "No surprises here. But as is often the case, some of the things we walk past every day can become big issues we simply don't see because they're always there."

"Here's a category that's fairly unique to today's corporate environment," Michael pointed out. "In the last five years, our intranet portal has become our primary source for internal information. What used to be distributed via paper reports or memos is now generally available only in electronic form.

"These days, if you call someone and ask for data, the standard answer will be, 'it's on the web.' You already knew that, of course, but wcrc asking since you *couldn't find it* on your own – because it was indexed in the third tier of someone's multi-layered drop down menu."

"I have that problem, too," Tony replied, "but since I am pretty much the keeper of my own information, I have to look in the mirror to complain about indexing … so what are you going to do about your problem?"

"We got lucky on this one," I said, "because we formed a small group to work on the issue. Many of these people were involved in the original construction of the internal site and feel some ownership for fixing what isn't working now."

"As a start," Michael added, "they are going to place a 'suggestion box' function on the intranet portal's front page so complaints and ideas for improvements can be easily collected for the team to work on.

"We debated about whether or not *Workload* deserved its own category," Michael continued. "In some respects, time and workload relate closely to the *Sheer Volume* topics. However, we think there could be totally different causes for the problem that warrant a separate look.

"So, this is one we are going to put aside and look at separately in each of our departments. There may be real workload balancing issues to be addressed, but there also may be some employees in need of time management training."

"It is a good idea to separate these issues," Tony observed. "Communications are only a part of the workload picture, and action on workload is something the supervisor and employee have to look at within the context of their own specific activities."

"Phone problems are another area we expected to hear about," I said, "and the list includes problems like long-winded callers, 'call me' voicemail messages that aren't actionable, calls not being returned on a timely basis ... all the usual complaints."

"These are fairly typical problems," Tony said, "yet, at the same time, they can be remarkably important. In many cases, phone concerns are fellow travelers with underlying issues of much greater importance, such as respect and trust.

"Let me give you an example: If I don't really respect you or your opinions, I'm likely to be a little lazy about returning your calls. This is another issue you can address, at least to some degree, through a staff meeting discussion and then learn if there are more fundamental issues at hand."

"We think these last two matters are best looked at together," I said, "because it's possible that their causes – and solutions – lie outside our departments.

"The first of the two topics fall, loosely, under the category of *Trust*

Issues. We're hearing from our people about people in other departments who have serious credibility problems, use hidden agendas and in some cases, even employ 'spy' tactics to pry into matters that are not their concern.

"We are calling the second area *Strategies and Tactics Issues* for now. Our people told us they felt various departments sometimes seem to be working at cross-purposes. This lack of alignment results in confusing and conflicting direction and communications."

Michael continued, "So, if or when we do ask for support in resolving these situations, we want to make sure we've fully exhausted the things we can do on our own.

"We're planning to meet with our bosses tomorrow afternoon to give them the complete download from the focus groups, brief them on our plans and give them a heads up on these sensitive matters. Kim is going to be in the meeting to provide HR perspectives and help us all think through how to deal with these touchy subjects."

"My first reaction to these is to say as Hippocrates or his contemporary Galen may have said, '*Primum non nocere*,' Tony began, "or in plain words:

First, Do No Harm.

"I strongly recommend you proceed cautiously. Not *timidly*, mind you – because this is a legitimate problem – but rather *carefully*.

"I don't know the lay of the land inside your company well enough to give you detailed advice, but I would think you will want to review the trust and strategy matters with your managers in a very careful manner.

"You don't want to give them the impression you're simply pointing fingers or trying to upload your problems to them without first taking a run at them yourselves. There are some things you can and should do before you think about escalation.

"On the trust front, some low-key but serious face-to-face work can help. Some of the same tools you would use to settle less important disputes can work here, as well.

"Encourage your team members to reach out to the people they are having trouble with to get past the limitations of e-mail and voicemail. Schedule a lunch conversation. Ask them to meet for coffee in the morning or simply drop into their office around quitting time. Just getting to know people can make a lot of these issues go away.

"For issues that *don't* go away, you'll need to take a look at these on a case-by-case basis. If there are other issues going on, you may need to get personally involved. Later, if you can't fix it, you can escalate the matter to your own boss."

"That makes sense to me," I said. "We definitely don't want to stir things up with our chain of command if it's something we can handle on our own."

Tony continued. "Here's another approach to the *Strategies and Tactics Issues* you may want to consider. At a minimum, it will demonstrate to your teams that you're listening.

"Suppose you arrange meetings with some of the departments your people have identified as having alignment issues. You set them up under the heading of 'Improving Communications' and build an agenda that would focus not only on how to best communicate, but also probe for areas where your business policies or practices may not completely match.

"Meetings like this will usually trigger coordination work between the two departments that will improve alignment and make life easier for your people. If this doesn't work, you still have the option of bringing your bosses into the picture if they are needed."

"Whew," said Michael. "I think you've just helped us step around another minefield."

"What you've said makes great sense to me too, Tony," I said, "and again, your support has brought us such a long way!"

"I am honored by your gratitude," Tony smiled, "but please don't forget – you owe ME nothing. Our deal is simply that you pass it on … and our deal is also to end on time, so we need to do two things fairly quickly."

"Let me guess," I said, "I bet the first item is to review this flip chart to make sure we didn't omit anything important."

"Right again," said Tony.

Here is how the chart looked at the end of our discussion:

Communications That Count
Tentative "Just Do Its"

➤ E-mail
  • Develop etiquette piece
  • Pursue better spam filter
  • Track volume to see if actions are effective
➤ Conduct informal Interpersonal skills training
➤ Meetings
  • Fix conference room scheduling system
  • Make sure conference rooms have supplies and equipment that
    is working
➤ Intranet Portal
  • Leverage support team to work on improvements

Other Actions

➤ First, Do No Harm
➤ Workload Management - look at separately, by department
➤ Trust - Encourage individual outreach - intervene only if corrections
  aren't possible at individual level
➤ Strategic Alignment - Schedule bi-lateral meetings to improve
  alignment

"The last item on today's agenda is to quickly give you some areas to work on for next week, Tony said. "You have the '*Guidelines for Communications That Count*' on your 'just do it' list, so how about bringing back a draft? Perhaps I can help you refine it."

"Perfect," I said, "because it's something high on our to-do list and we need to get started."

"It's going to be a great day," said Michael, as the trio walked to the door and found the clouds had all but disappeared. "In fact, it already is!"

*　　*　　*

Here's what I put in my notebook for the day, along with copies of the flip chart's content:

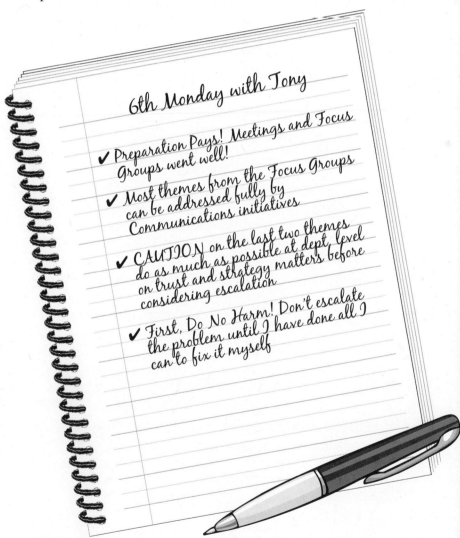

6th Monday with Tony

✓ Preparation Pays! Meetings and Focus Groups went well!

✓ Most themes from the Focus Groups can be addressed fully by Communications initiatives

✓ CAUTION on the last two themes do as much as possible at dept. level on trust and strategy matters before considering escalation

✓ First, Do No Harm! Don't escalate the problem until I have done all I can to fix it myself

The Seventh Monday

Right Enough
the First Time

I was really upbeat the next Monday morning! Michael and I had enjoyed an unusually productive week and had completed our homework by quitting time Friday.

"So, a good weekend?" Tony inquired as we came up the walk.

"Yes sir," I responded, "We're closing in on a pretty good plan and better yet, we had our homework finished on Friday so I was able to take the weekend off!"

"Mine was incredible, too," Michael chimed in, "and even though I wasn't on the clock, I picked up a great example of a clear and concise message for us to discuss.

"My youngest brother got married on Saturday, and my wife and I rode to the reception with my parents. My father was rehearsing his toast to the newlyweds in the car and when he had it down pat, I asked my mother what she was going to say."

"Michael," she said, "years ago, my own mother gave me great advice about what the Mother of the Groom is supposed to do … and that is to avoid upstaging the bride's mother or drawing attention away from the newlyweds. It's really simple and easy to remember: Show up, shut up and wear beige!"

 We laughed our way into Tony's kitchen, filled our coffee cups and were soon at work.

"We tried to follow your advice as we put together the centerpiece of our homework," I began. "We've studied the data we gathered from the focus groups, notes from our sessions with you, and did a quick draft of guidelines that might be needed.

"Next, we reviewed it with some of the best communicators we have on our teams, plus some excellent wordsmiths from the Advertising and PR departments, and picked up more good ideas. Finally, we edited it ruthlessly to get it down to something that will fit on a single piece of paper we could present as a single screen on our intranet portal.

"But before we show you this page, I want to talk about how we plan to roll this out. Because this information is so important, we're planning a live meeting with all hands. We want to be able to demonstrate our belief that the *Communications That Count* **can** make a major difference in the quality of our work – and the quality of our work life.

"Most of what we will have to say won't be a tough sell, but by going live we have an opportunity to head off problems at the pass, so to speak. We don't want people just reading a memo and then grumping about something we could easily address," I explained.

"We'll have some – not all – of the supporting tools ready to go," Michael continued. "We'll have them in paper form to hand out at the meeting, but the long-term resource will be the intranet portal. Hot links from key words in the one-page guidelines piece will take the user directly to more details, job aids and examples.

"So," I said, "we're hoping you'll find this totally self-explanatory, with the caveat that the hot link materials aren't there."

Communications That Count...

...have clear objectives. They are designed to cause action, to convey key information and/or to change or reinforce others' thinking.

Our Goals:

1. More communications that go out *right enough the first time*
2. Better effectiveness and productivity
3. Reduced overall message volume, workload and stress

You Touch it, You Own it

♦ **Senders** are *primarily* responsible for the effectiveness of communications.
♦ **Receivers** are responsible for identifying problems – it is **not** okay to ignore items you don't understand.
♦ **Management** is responsible for systemic issues and availability of common information.

Guidelines

Effective *Communications That Count*:
    ♦ have an evident business purpose and specific objectives
    ♦ are clear, concise and direct
    ♦ use the most effective and efficient medium for delivery
    ♦ include the appropriate people
    ♦ use a courteous, positive, businesslike tone
    ♦ are complete, correct and fully thought-through
    ♦ provide clear motivation for action for all involved

The *Reporter's Questions* are your friends. Does your communication have answers to the "who, what when, why, how, where and how much" questions?

Go Slow To Go Fast

"Not bad," Tony said when he had completed his review. "I can immediately see how this is going to work as the anchor for your program. Now tell me a little about what you're planning to have on the other end of the hot links."

"As I mentioned earlier, we'll have several resources to support this page," I explained. "There will be more than one way to get to the information – like most good web resources. We'll have hot links from keywords on the front page leading directly to related entries, plus we'll have a set of conventional menus by subject.

"For example, we'll have a 'Definitions' section that will include a glossary of terms and acronyms we use in CTC (*Communications That Count*) materials. This section also will include expanded explanations of concepts, such as the difference between objectives and desired outcomes."

"But wait, there's more," Michael said, sounding strangely like a late-night infomercial announcer. "The 'Tools' section will contain all kinds of job aids and checklists, such as my little helper on objectives, an e-mail etiquette checklist and your meeting preparation worksheet.

"Another section will be called 'Templates and Samples.' This will provide standard versions of the communications we prepare every day, such as outlines for customer letters. It will also offer layouts for concept papers, project status reports, budget requests and so on."

"And finally," I said, "the hot links will include a 'Resources' section including a bibliography, links to external resources and a training menu. Within the training menu, a link will lead to HR for the formal courses and an internal connection will connect to materials for the informal sessions we're planning."

"As you can imagine, a lot of this material comes straight out of here," Michael added, pointing to his Mondays with Tony notebook. "But some will come from other sources, such as our own files for the standard letters and from the websites you recommended for some of the checklists. Others are still in the development phase."

"Like this one," I said, "that we're struggling with now. We could use your help on working up something we're calling a 'media picker' job aid.

"Our plan was to summarize the characteristics of various media – their positives and negatives – with a recommendation as to what each is best suited for. For example, here's what we might say about e-mail communications:

Media	Characteristics	Positives	Negatives	Best for
E-mail	• Indirect • Not interactive • Not location dependent	• Allows time shifts • Fast • Efficient	• Can be cold • Not fully private	• Straightforward, fact-based matters

"The problem is this – when you stack up all the media choices available, you wind up with a huge chart no one will use, but we need to convey this information in some form because it represents an important part of our problem."

"Hmmm," murmured Tony, studying the e-mail chart. "I see what you mean. How about starting with a simple list of 'do's and don'ts?'" This could raise consciousness on frequently-occurring problems in this area ... but then again, some of the most important and critical errors may not be all that frequent.

"Maybe you could take a two-pronged approach," he suggested. "You could plan another short staff meeting and use a PowerPoint™ presentation to walk through the descriptions you put on the big chart. By showing them on a screen, one at a time, I think you can avoid scaring people off.

"Most of your guidelines would be common sense and people probably don't need a chart to remember those – but they do need to hear from you about the importance of using the right media and the consequences that can result from carelessness."

"Great idea," I said. "How about building the list right now?"

"You got it," Tony said as he rose to get the flip chart and markers. "Okay, let's get to work. I like to start with the 'don'ts.' In my experience, even though I preach a positive approach, negatives often do a better job of grabbing someone's attention."

We quickly filled a chart with all the "don'ts" we could think of:

Communications That Count
Media Selection Don'ts

➤ Don't put anything in an e-mail or on the intranet that you wouldn't like to see published on the front page of the newspaper.

➤ Don't use meetings for matters that can be best handled by individuals (group writing, for example, is very wasteful).

➤ Don't overuse Instant Messaging – each one you send is an immediate interruption to the receiver.

➤ Don't depend on the intranet portal to communicate urgent matters. People need to be alerted by phone or e-mail if something is hot.

➤ Don't use telephone calls for discussions that require visual references without sending graphics or data via e-mail in advance.

"Good list," said Michael, "and now we can move on to the positives."

We repeated the process and came up with the following list of positive suggestions:

Communications That Count
Media Selection Do's

➤ Do use face-to-face contacts for sensitive, emotional or personal topics.

➤ Do use meetings when collaboration and diverse views are important to generate better solutions and plans.

➤ Do use E-mail for straightforward, fact-based matters – it can save a lot of time vs. phone calls or meetings.

➤ Do use the Intranet Portal to post reports and information, and keep your postings up to date.

➤ Do use the telephone for matters that require a high degree of interaction. One short call often can do the job of six e-mails.

"This is a good start," Tony said after re-reading both lists, "and I think you can use these to begin your staff meeting. Then let your team help identify other issues.

"Now, let's spend a few minutes talking about how you can avoid the 'starchy' feel when you present this to your teams."

"Well, first of all," Michael began, "we decided to carry the 'Meatball Surgery' idea into the meeting to help make the point about 'right enough the first time.' We haven't worked out the final details yet and thought you might like to help."

"Great," said Tony. "This is the fun part and I have been thinking about it since our first discussion.

"How about using some of the elements from M*A*S*H to theme the meeting? You could go to the Army surplus store and pick up used fatigue jackets for yourselves and any others who will be presenting. If your budget permits, get a supply of olive drab t-shirts for your team members. This doesn't have to be expensive – you just need a few stage-setters to make the connection with M*A*S*H.

"Michael, you could list yourself on the agenda as 'Hawkeye' and bill Jeni as Major Houlihan, as long as Jeni can put up with the 'hot lips' fallout that might follow!

"Depending on how you want to cast others – assuming they have a strong sense of humor – you could use characters like Radar, Father Mulcahy and Major Burns to spice up your meeting," Tony pointed out.

"There are all kinds of things we can tie into this theme, I added enthusiastically, "and I have some people who will be delighted to work on this – and who can keep their mouths shut so the surprise isn't ruined. You can come too, Tony, if you'd like wear the Inspector General's outfit!"

"I might just take you up on that ... just make my fatigue jacket a large and spell the name P-E-A-R-C-E to avoid confusion with the other Pierce at the front of the room."

We were all obviously pleased with the potential of the M*A*S*H tie-in.

"Well, once again, we've managed to use up our time together in what seemed to me just an instant, and as usual, our outputs are really very good," said Tony, gathering the papers we had worked with during the session.

"Our next meeting is Monday number eight … and this is when you'll be getting your final ticket punch, so here's one last homework assignment.

"What I'm going to assign requires a little visioning, a little planning and some program development work. I'd like you to leap ahead to six months out, and picture what success your current efforts have achieved – individually and to the entire organization.

"Then comes what, perhaps, may be the hard part. Tell me what you're going to do differently to maintain the progress you've made and how you plan to move on to yet a higher level of communications effectiveness."

*　　*　　*

Along with the Do's and Don'ts from the flip charts, here is what I put in my spiral notebook for the day:

7th Monday with Tony

✔ Goals-Roles-Guidelines are right on!

✔ Leveraging Intranet Portal is Key

✔ Use M*A*S*H cues to theme the team meeting and to introduce the "Meatball Surgery" approach in communications

✔ Emphasize that goal is not perfection, but to be more effective by being "Right Enough the First Time"

The Eighth Monday
Dr. Seuss was Right

As we walked up the steps to Tony's door for the last of our meetings, Michael and I were having mixed emotions – excited about what we had accomplished and yet sad this would be our last meeting with Tony.

 To keep things on the lighter side, once Tony had greeted us, Michael started our day off with a joke and we laughed our way to the coffee pot.

Michael was the first to speak on this final day with Tony. "I can easily work our plan, but haven't yet figured out just exactly where I should be going with this thing on a longer term basis."

"I'm with Michael on that," I said, "especially

because the training wheels get kicked out from under us today. I'll also be the first to admit, there are still facets to the communications picture I frankly don't understand, yet I feel I should – and I really don't see a way to get that done anytime soon.

"Going back to that 'Meatball Surgery' analogy," Michael continued. "Let's think a minute about where those doctors were going. Because they were stuck in Korea for the duration, they needed to continue to improve their skills so they could save more lives in the time they had. Yet, they also had to build the skills that would be needed when they returned to the real world where the 'right enough the first time' wouldn't be appropriate … **and**, they had to maintain their sanity **and** provide leadership to their teams while they rode it out. Not a simple challenge."

"Our lot in life looks a little easier than that," I said.

"Yes," said Michael, "and Tony's been through this before…."

"Indeed I have" Tony said, settling into his chair. "But before we get into some of our heavier discussions for today, I'd like to take a moment to put our meetings into perspective.

"Some would say we're coming to the end of the road, since this is our last Monday together, but I see it quite differently. I think we're simply at a fork, where we will each go off in our own directions and begin new legs on our journeys."

"Leave it to Tony to anticipate the central question I had for this morning," Michael said. "We're clearly starting on a whole new path, but we're looking for some tips, based on your travels."

"Well, I have some for you, and we'll get into them as soon as we can clear out your homework."

"But wait," Michael said. "Before we get into the real work, we wanted to make sure there was time for a little presentation we need to make."

"Right," I said, and produced a small box from my briefcase. "You know it is really hard to find just the right gift to express how we feel ... so we settled on something at least we knew you could use."

Inside the box was a pound of premium coffee beans from Colombia, a subscription to the International Coffee of the Month Club, and a special mug in an unmistakable shade of Army fatigue green.

The card was inscribed to Tony with the message "With our undying gratitude and best wishes," and signed, "Your favorite meatballs."

"You two are absolutely too much! You couldn't have picked a better memento, and I'll think of you each time I brew up some of your special coffee. I have something for you, too, but you'll have to wait until we get our work done! Ready to get started?"

"In terms of a vision for the near future," I began, "we couldn't find a crystal ball, but we did work out what we believe are reasonable expectations for the next four to six months.

"In order to set goals and to know whether we've made progress, we're going use the team survey we used several weeks ago as a baseline for measuring effectiveness. We'll resurvey at 60 and 120 days to see if we've moved the needle.

"On the volume issue, we're going to ask people to keep manual logs of their volumes for a couple of weeks at the beginning of our program and then again later when we do the follow-up surveys. We won't be able to count every kind of communication, but we think this will cover the most important areas where volume was an issue."

"Moving on to where we'd like to be," Michael continued, "we believe our plans support a significant improvement. So, a reasonable goal would be to move up our average effectiveness scores by about two points or more and to cut overall volume by about 20 percent.

"Here's a small version of the sign we've put up on our walls:

Just Do It Communications Goals
Two Point + Improvement in Effectiveness with 20% Less Volume

"We're not going to set reduction targets for individual types of communications because we actually expect some to go up, and our mix will definitely be different down the road.

"As far as the effectiveness targets, this method of measurement – asking people about their own numbers – probably isn't super accurate, but will be 'right enough,'" Michael explained. "This isn't an engineering exercise so it isn't extremely precise, but for monitoring purposes, we just want to see if we've made a significant dent in the communications problem … and we're pretty confident we will."

"We also think our action plan will drive improvements big

enough for everyone on the team to recognize," I said, "and for all to enjoy at least some improvement in their quality of work life."

"You're right to not set overly aggressive goals," Tony observed, "because you have to consider the full gamut of talent and motivation you're working with. But at the same time, I think you need to talk to some of your star players about setting the bar considerably higher, so you'll come out of this phase with some huge individual success stories."

"Good point," said Michael, "and Jeni and I need to stretch, as well."

"Moving on to the second part of our assignment – maintaining momentum," I said, "we've put it into a pretty simple 'do more / do less / continue' format."

Do More
♦ Use more care in our personal communications to assure we always set a positive example.
♦ Add measurements – tracking of e-mail and phone volume, etc.
♦ Monitor intranet portal usage and survey satisfaction regularly.
♦ Work with individuals who may have special needs through coaching and counseling. Identify training needs for specific skill improvements.
Do Less
♦ Reduce our own "hot reactions" and coach/counsel individuals with difficulties in this area to reduce theirs. End the "border wars" instead of starting new ones.
♦ Do less finger pointing. The "You touch it, you own it" philosophy will become a way of life.
Continue
♦ Continue to be the best leaders we can be, and help our teams work through this challenge.

"I would guess," Tony began, "your individual plans have some added details. For example, in addition to personally taking the training courses you'll be offering to your team, are you planning to do some independent studies and self-development work?"

"Yes," I said, "and this brings us back to Michael's questions about where we should be headed. How deep of a dive do we take into this thing called communications? How high is up?"

"If you had asked me this several weeks ago," Tony began, "you wouldn't have been ready for the answer, and candidly, I'm not sure I would have given you the same advice I would give you now. Back then, you didn't have a solid grip on how important these *Communications That Count* really are.

"To give you a look down the road, I want to show you this diagram again – the one where there are two main components that drive communications effectiveness.

"Again, **Preparedness** covers everything you need to do just short of opening your mouth or pushing the send button on an e-mail.

"**Delivery** is the actual communication event, whether it's a letter, a phone call or a speech. When we add two factors together, we get **Effectiveness** – the extent to which you achieve your communications objectives.

"If you develop consistency in your communications efforts and can continually be in the upper right quadrant, you'll achieve most of your objectives. You'll also be in what I call the *Communications Mastery* zone, earning an amazing payoff.

"By being consistently better, even by a very small increment in effectiveness, your communications will achieve a higher impact. You'll get what you want. People will support your agendas enthusiastically. You'll be respected and trusted ... and you'll make it look easy.

"Notice I said 'make it look easy,' not 'it's easy to do.' As you already know, just dealing with the English language with all its rules and exceptions is difficult enough. Add the complexities of each medium, each topic, each audience, each objective and you have puzzles that can't be solved even by a Super Computer.

"I'll also add that *Mastery* can be a very temporary thing because the *Mastery* advantage is never absolute – it's all about getting disproportionate rewards for being just a bit better than others. So retaining *Master* status involves continuing to stay at least a half step ahead of the sheriff, so to speak.

"You are at a gateway," Tony pointed out, "and whether or not you choose to take up the *Mastery* challenge, I wish you well." He then handed us each a handsome hardbound book and said, "This has some good tricks of the trade you can use along the way, regardless of the path you choose."

We thanked Tony effusively for his help and guidance, and reaffirmed our commitment to pass along what he had shared with us. As he walked us to the door he reminded us, "This is not good bye, but rather farewell – enjoy your journey!"

To seal my commitments in the manner Tony recommended, I put a copy of my "Do More – Do Less – Continue" List in my Monday Morning notebook as soon as I got to the office and added these entries:

8th Monday with Tony

✔ Consistently high levels of Preparation and Delivery get you consistent levels of communication effectiveness

✔ High levels of consistent effectiveness get you to the Communications Mastery Zone

✔ Being "in the zone" means my communications will have higher impact, I'll get more done ... and earn more respect in the process

✔ I'm going for it – Communications Mastery can be a major tool in my leadership toolbox!

At lunch, I picked a solo seat in a quiet corner of the cafeteria and took out the book Tony had given us.

Its title was *Life is a Series of Presentations* and Tony's inscription in my copy looked like this:

Jeni:

Here's a quote from a favorite author that fits your situation perfectly! Congratulations!

> Today is your day.
> You're off to Great Places!
> You're off and away!
>
> You have brains in your head.
> You have feet in your shoes
> You can steer yourself any direction you choose.
>
> You're on your own.
> And you know what you know.
> And YOU are the one who'll decide where to go.
>
> From: Oh, the Places you'll go!
> By Dr. Seuss

All the best!
Tony

Epilogue

*P*resent Day…

The plan we developed with Tony's help is working. Since Michael and I implemented it six months ago, our results have improved dramatically and we are able to address other issues. Our team is working better together and I think everyone agrees that our improved communication has made this a much better place to work.

Michael recently began his second round of internal communication seminars, just as he promised Tony. He conducts them in the cafeteria on Monday mornings and, as expected, he attracts a capacity crowd each week.

I am grateful to be able to learn from Tony. My career has skyrocketed, as I was recently promoted to replace Jeff, who is leading a new division. Fulfilling my promise to Tony, I did find the book within me – you're holding the finished product.

As for Tony – he and his wife are exploring parts of Asia they have never seen, including a stop where the story of the 4077th M*A*S*H was set. When he returns, Tony will be working on a new book and juggling speaking engagements around the country. He asked us to keep in touch and said when we come to visit he'll have the hot coffee waiting!

Most people don't have – and never will have – the luxury of a mentor like Tony. My desire is that you will be able to learn from him and pass on this knowledge to others.

Bonus Communications Tips

E-mail

1. Use the subject line to flag your topic or desired action. Use "urgent," "hot" or "help" when appropriate but don't overuse.

2. Keep e-mails to one screen and one subject whenever possible. To get a quick response, be brief in your request.

3. Make your e-mails "easy-read." Use bulleted phrases, numbered lists and short, separated paragraphs.

4. Create a standard signature that inserts automatically and contains your full name, title, phone number and other contact information.

5. Use auto-responders when you will be away for a day or longer.

6. Don't respond in anger – save a draft and review later.

7. Keep your inbox clean and create folders to organize messages you'll keep. Delete items you don't really need.

8. Use CC's only when you're sure the recipient really needs or wants to know.

9. NEVER forward chain letters – they cause stress and aggravation.

10. A personal note can have great power. When a phone call would be best, make it.

Telephone

1. When connected, confirm it's a good time to talk. Make it clear how much time you need – the famous "gotta minute" can be a red flag.

2. State the purpose of the call and identify key desired outcomes.

3. Start on your agenda without delay, and launch with words like this: "Let's begin with the Smith Account matter – what's your take on ...."

4. Take deep breaths to allow the other person to "get in." Pauses are okay and can encourage the other person to say something you can react to if it's an objection.

5. Stay focused on the important items. For other items, wait until near the end of the call if time permits or to be handled off-line later.

6. Listen carefully. Close each item and confirm agreements before moving on.

7. Recap and Confirm. At the end of your call, recap your outcomes on each and reconfirm agreement.

8. End Promptly. If you have something else you need to do, just say so in a courteous way: "I have another meeting beginning in X minutes and have to prepare, so I need to say goodbye for now or ...."

9. Immediately after the call, put your notes from the call in an e-mail to the other person to seal agreements and set timing for follow-up actions.

10. Schedule a call (for complex matters or long discussions) via e-mail or drop a voicemail asking the person to call you at a time convenient to them between x and y.

Better Presentation Effectiveness through Preparation and Delivery

Ten Ways to Improve Your Preparedness

1. Do not present until you understand your audicncc and know enough about the subject to be viewed as "qualified."

2. Make time to develop clear objectives and a timed agenda.

3. Plan Ahead. Identify material and equipment needed early

4. Select a room and layout that is the right size and shape for your group.

5. Send the agenda and key information to the audience in advance.

6. Check all materials for Tone, Spelling, Readability, Structure and Conciseness.

7. Rehearse. Assure pronunciations are correct and confirm timing for reveal of slides or other visual aids.

8. Prepare for Contingencies. Have backup data on hand. Be ready for questions and timing issues (e.g. running too long).

9. Solicit Comments. Use feedback to continuously improve

10. Use checklists. Reminders help assure that all gets done.

Ten Ways to Improve Your Delivery

1. Assure all materials & equipment are available. Check sight lines and lighting to assure the audience can see you and your visuals and do a sound and equipment check.

2. Meet with hosts and greet audience members as they arrive to help establish rapport.

3. Use a strong opening to explain your "Purpose, Process and Payoff" to connect your objectives and the benefits to the audience, and briefly review your agenda.

4. Have someone known to the audience introduce you or make statements about your qualifications or preparation for the presentation.

5. Relax, speak clearly and modulate volume/tone of voice appropriately for audience. Align body language with message. Smile and maintain eye contact with audience.

6. Get and maintain engagement by using humor and interactive elements.

7. Follow your agenda, but maintain flexibility to respond to audience needs.

8. Clearly ask the audience to support your objective, and confirm agreement by asking for direct feedback.

9. Recap. Review agreements, desired next steps and action plans to bring closure to the session.

10. End on Time.

ACKNOWLEDGEMENTS

A word of thanks to many people
that helped make this book possible:

Alice Adams
Tawnya Austin
Sara Bowling
Marti Brigman
Kristin Campbell
Nonie Jobe
Greg Kaiser
Marj Lowe
Melissa Monogue

About the Authors

David Cottrell, is an internationally-known leadership consultant, educator, and speaker. His business experience includes senior management positions with Xerox and FedEx. David's 25-plus years of professional experience are reflected in eighteen highly acclaimed books including the perennial best sellers *Monday Morning Leadership* and *Listen Up, Leader.* To contact David, visit **www.cornerstoneleadership.com.**

Tony Jeary is a conference speaker, strategic facilitator, and success coach, helping others be their best. His company, Tony Jeary High-Performance Resources, offers private coaching, speaking, and strategic planning, as well as unique resources based on the subject of *Presentation Mastery*™. Most are specifically linked to his best selling book, *Life is a Series of Presentations.* To contact Tony visit **www.tonyjeary.com** or 1-877-2 INSPIRE.

George Lowe is a co-author with Tony Jeary on *We've Got to Stop Meeting Like This!, Meeting Magic* and an upcoming *Presentation Mastery* title. He is President of Lowe & Associates. Lowe offers a range of consulting and communications services with special focus on communications strategy, presentation development and meeting design. He established his business in June 2000, following over 30 years with Ford Motor Company, where he held a variety of leadership positions in the U.S. and Mexico. Contact George at: georgelowe@ameritech.net.

Six ways to bring
Presentation Mastery™ and Strategic Effectiveness
to your team:

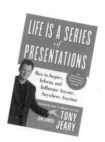

1. Keynote/Conference Speaker
Tony Jeary's keynotes and speeches are energizing, entertaining and educational. Tony will accelerate your success by increasing your sales, help you become more persuasive, and save time by using proven processes. Visit www.tonyjeary.com.

2. Strategic Facilitator/Success Coach:
Tony can help your group or initiative focus more clearly on strategic goals and objectives, develop and deepen a resonant brand clarify and help you design your core message. Many of the world's top CEOs have chosen Tony Jeary as their success coach. www.tonyjeary.com.

3. *Life is a Series of Presentations*
This dynamic book will teach you how to persuade people to get the results you want. You will discover how to involve and engage your audience for maximum buy-in and tailor the presentation to keep your audience focused and absorb your message. $12.95 at www.cornerstoneleadership.com

4. Life is a Series of Presentations Success Theater
Experience this interactive DVD session that teach the key elements featured in *Life is a Series of Presentations*. Review it time and time again to continually improve your presentation effectiveness. www.tonyjeary.com

5. Life is a Series of Presentations Video Training
This video will show you how to master your presentation skills and accelerate your success. www.tonyjeary.com

6. Monday Morning Communications PowerPoint Presentation
This professional presentation is ready to present to your team. Download the presentation today at www.cornerstoneleadership.com. $79.95

For information on these and other products,
visit www.tonyjeary.com or call 877-2-INSPIRE

Recommended Resources

Monday Morning Leadership is David Cottrell's best-selling book. It offers unique encouragement and direction that will help you become a better manager, employee, and person. $12.95

The Manager's Communication Handbook will allow you to connect with employees and create the understanding, support and acceptance critical to your success. $9.95

Meeting Magic is a powerful handbook to help make your meetings productive. $9.95

Inspire Any Audience has over 200 pages of tools and tips to help you get action from your audience. (Hardcover) $29.95

Too Many Emails contains dozens of tips and techniques to increase your email effectiveness and efficiency. $9.95

Life is a Series of Presentations will teach you how to persuade people to get the results you want. (Hardcover) $23.95

136 Effective Presentation Tips is a powerful handbook providing 136 easy-to-use tips to make every presentation a success. $9.95

175 Ways to Get More Done in Less Time has 175 great tips on how to get things done faster and better. $9.95

12 Choices ... That Lead to Your Success is about success ... how to achieve it, keep it and enjoy it ... by making better choices. $14.95

You and Your Network is profitable reading for those who want to learn how to develop healthy relationships with others. $9.95

Monday Morning Communications **PowerPoint Presentation** This professional presentation is ready to present to your team. Download the presentation today at www.cornerstoneleadership.com. $79.95

Visit www.**cornerstoneleadership**.com
for additional books and resources.